A Mother's Love
A Son's Regret

ISBN: 9781973209119

Written By
Corey Porter

A Mother's Love A Son's Regret

As a child, I was disrespectful. Words like shut-up, you make me sick, and I hate you had become included in my daily vocabulary. I would often tell her she was annoying. Showing off while my friends were present for laughs, as I would say to her, "get out of my room!" I felt empowered, grown, cool which is everything a teen wants to feel like.

I would often forget her birthday. She never reminded me, so I treated it like it was just another day.

I don't know what made her so annoying to me. Oh wait, I remember. My mother would always try to correct or change me. She would say, "Don't hang around this person, or don't hang around that person." The lectures were never-ending. My mother would say, "Don't smoke this, or don't drink that." She would ask, "Did you do your homework? Did you fill out more job applications today?" It was a dream of mine that one day I wouldn't have to hear her voice every morning, nagging and complaining.

She would always leave me notes on the refrigerator, reminding me of everything I thought I already knew. She would write, "Do the dishes, clean your room, take out the garbage, LOOK FOR A JOB; I Left you $10 on the kitchen table."
She would also sign
"Mom Loves You" and encourage me to read Exodus 20:12.

I knew it was a Bible scripture, but I never opened the Bible to see what Exodus 20:12 read. I thought the Bible was for old people.
I never reciprocated my love for her.
I'm sure she knew I loved her.
I mean, I am her son, right?
She had to know my love for her.

Now what I'm about to tell you changed my life forever. At the time, I was 19 years of age, driving with some friends I had known since high school. One of my friends in the car told us about someone who owed him money for the weed he had sold them. He was saying, "When I see him, I'm killing him!"

A Mother's Love A Son's Regret

We laughed it off and never thought anything else about it. We were just some immature teens with our whole lives ahead of us.

We arrived at a stop sign next to a gas station. One of my friends driving with us says to the other friend, "Is that the kid who owes you money? He's standing right there!" "Yeah, that's him! Let me out of the car," he said. We all sat in the car with excitement, thinking we were about to see a fight.

My friend walks towards the kid, never saying a word. He pulls out a gun and shoots the kid once in the head. "BANG!!!!!" The kid falls to the ground. Blood began flowing out of his head, mouth, and nose. My friend runs back to the car, yelling, "Drive! Drive! Drive!" It was pure chaos in that car. Everybody was yelling and screaming, except for me. I was speechless. No words would come out of my mouth. I was in shock.

The driver of the car was now driving 80 mph, running red lights, and stop signs.

Corey Porter

I told them, "Let me out of the car!"
I walked for 3 hours crying profusely.
Police were driving throughout the city
frantically. The sound of sirens was the
only sound you could hear. "He murdered
that kid", I kept repeating to myself.

When I finally got home, my mother was
lying on the sofa watching the news.
My eyes were now dry but still red from
crying.
My mother says, "I'm so glad you're
home. A young kid was just murdered by
the gas station." She covered her mouth,
shaking her head as she watched the
news reporter at the scene of the crime. "I
Feel horrible for that young man's
mother," my mother softly said to herself.
I began to walk up the stairs towards my
room, and my mother says, "I see your
eyes. Don't bring that garbage into my
house!" She assumed my eyes were red
from smoking weed, not knowing I was
crying.

I stayed in my room the entire night.
I felt scared and nervous as my stomach
rumbled.

A Mother's Love A Son's Regret

It was 3:06 in the morning when I heard the repeated banging on the door. Bang! Bang!! BANG!! "Open up! It's the Police!" My mother grabs her house robe and runs to see who is banging violently on our door. "How can I help you, officer?", my mother nervously asked. One of the 6 police officers who were standing on our porch asked, "Ma'am is your son home?" "Yes, what is this about?", my mother asked. "Ma'am, your son was involved in a homicide", the police officer replied.

The scream that my mother let out was like a sound I've never heard. It sounded like agonizing pain. The officers handcuffed me and led me to the police car, where I was arrested and charged with second-degree murder.

I was held in the county jail for 6 months before my trial started. Those were long anxious months. While in the county jail, I remember seeing my friend who was responsible for committing the murder. He was charged with second-degree murder as well. I remember him saying to me, "Don't snitch. If we all keep quiet, we'll all go home." I agreed, and I never saw him again until our trial.

After 6 long months of waiting, I finally had a trial date. The trial took 4 weeks, and my mother was there every day. She spent all of her savings to get me a lawyer. I appreciated her. I mistreated my mother most of my life, yet she was the only one in the courtroom there to support me. I felt ashamed, and I didn't deserve her love. I've told her I hated her. I've told her I wished she were dead.
I've disrespected her in so many ways, and yet she sat in that courtroom just for me. She told me time after time, "Don't hang around this person or don't hang around that person." "Don't smoke this, or don't drink that." At that moment, I could hear all her warnings clear as I sat with my life in the judge's hands.

The verdict was in. "GUILTY!"
My so-called friend who actually committed the murder implicated the rest of us for a lesser sentence.
I was sentenced to 15 years in prison for a murder my friend committed. My

mother's heart was in pieces. I was selfish. I never knew my actions would cause her so much pain. Weeks would turn into months, months into years, and my mother would visit me every weekend. She would bring me money for the commissary. Each day another letter would arrive at the prison for me. It would be my mother encouraging me to stay focused and out of trouble. We would play spades and UNO every time she would visit. Photos of us laughing hung on the wall of my cell. As we ate chips and microwavable sandwiches, we would imagine the day I left this dreadful place. I watched my mother's hair turn from black to white as years would come and go. One day, when she came to visit me, I said,

"Ma, I love you more than life. I'm sorry for being an ungrateful, horrible son. I've put you through so much pain and sorrow because I was too stupid to listen. I don't deserve the love you have shown me my entire life. Forgive me, Ma. Please forgive and forget all of the horrible things I've said to you. I love you, Ma."

She replied, *"I've forgiven you a long time ago. You see, son, I only wanted what was best for you. I only wanted you to become the best person you can possibly be. I never wanted to annoy you or make you angry, but I will never stop being your mother. I will never stop telling you what is right and what is wrong. I love you, son. If it took 10 years in prison for you to recognize what true love looks like, then It was all worth it."*

On May 23rd, 2003, I was released from prison after serving 13 years. I was 32 years old. My mother was standing there as I walked out of that prison with her arms open wide.
That small old lady with glasses and white hair never gave up on me. Now I know what Exodus 20:12 said in the Bible.

"Honor your father and your mother, so that you may live long in the land the Lord your God is giving you."- Exodus 20:12

I eventually went on to graduate from

college in 2008 with a creative writing degree. The day I walked across that stage was the proudest day of not only my life but my mother's as well.

8 Years Later

You would think after building a strong bond with my mother we lived happily ever after. You would imagine I would cherish every moment with her from now on, but life doesn't work that way. One thing I can assure you is that freedom can bring about amnesia to a man once incarcerated. Prison is all about survival. A man will literally do and say anything to survive his time in prison.

I've seen men pretend to be in love with 3 different women just to maintain frequent visitation. These women had no idea they were being used and manipulated. I've seen young men on the visiting floor hugging and kissing women that could easily be their grandmother. A visit to an inmate was like a Christmas gift, and some would do anything to get one. You'll love whoever will put money in your commissary and send you monthly packages. This is life behind prison walls.

I'm a free man now. I've graduated college, and I wish I could tell you that I'm making a ton of money in my new career, but I instead will tell you the truth.
I've been unemployed since my graduation in 2008.
You can go to school and get as many degrees as you want, but if you have a felony, that's the only title jobs pay attention to. All I wanted was a second chance at life and to do things right this time. Unfortunately, regrets and mistakes follow some of us our entire lives like a shadow.

It was now 2011. I was a 40-year old man still living at home with his mother.
I felt like a 19-year old all over again.
My mother still would leave me money on the kitchen table every morning before she went to work.
The constant daily questions about my job search and relationship status had become unbearable at times. My mother didn't understand how hard it was to start a new successful life when you were

constantly reminded of your past. I admit, sometimes I would just sit back on the sofa and watch TV all day with absolutely no plans of looking for a job.

Some people clean when they are angry, while others would go shopping when they're upset. I guess I found peace in watching funny shows on TV.

I was just a 40-year-old loser who still lived at home with his 65-year-old mother. What woman with dignity and respect for herself would want a guy like me?

Life is a no-nonsense teacher. There are thousands of men in prison today whose only crime was being at the wrong place and at the wrong time. Men who had careers, families, and the potential to be something great are sitting in lonely prison cells because they've chosen the wrong friends.

I encourage every young man reading this to know who your true friends are and to be aware of your surroundings at all times. Surround yourself with goal-oriented people who have the ambition to be great. Life is all about choices.

My mother and my relationship began to fall apart. We would argue and yell some days, and other days we'd be distant and quiet with each other. She thought I could just wake up, submit my resume, and I'll get a call back from a manager saying, "You're hired!" She had no idea about the life of an ex-convict. She accused me of being lazy and procrastinating, which made me angry.

One day, while we were arguing, I became disrespectful. I recall telling her to shut up and get out of my face. She looked at me and said, "Oh, you're back to being 19 again?" I hated the fact that I let my anger cause me to revert back to my disrespectful ways.

"I'm sorry, Ma," I said as I walked back to my room. I just wish she understood my frustration. I needed her to know that this time I wanted to be successful just as much as she wanted me to be.

Week after week, I went on job interviews, all ending with the exact words, "We'll be in touch." I knew that was a code word for we're not hiring a felon.

Soon I began to give up on job

searching. I found myself eating and watching TV every day for what seemed like months. I gained 20 pounds, my hair hadn't been cut for a long time, and I began to come to the realization that I may be living with my mother forever. I just didn't care anymore.

This is where things began to unravel. One night, I was sitting at a bar alone, drinking and thinking, when I felt a tap on my shoulder. I turned to see who it was, and it was one of my friends who were in the car with me that regretful day the murder occurred. He had been home since 2005 and seemed to be doing well for himself.

He told me he worked construction and was married with two kids. I smiled and continued to congratulate, but I was jealous and envious, to be completely honest. How did things work out so well for him, and I'm still living at home with my mother?

I already knew he would ask me what I've been doing, so I planned the perfect lie in my head. Surprisingly, he never asked. Could he tell that I was struggling in all aspects of my life? If I weren't so proud and jealous, I could have asked him to connect me with the construction gig he was doing. Emotions will always cloud your better judgment. My friend and I concluded our conversation then went our separate ways. I watched as he walked towards his new BMW and drove away as if he were in a commercial. We both were in prison, but somehow he'd gotten his second chance at life while my search continued.

As I walked home, that day tears rolled down my face. "God, what am I doing wrong? Why haven't you granted me my second chance?", I said as I looked to the clouds. I didn't understand why my life was still at a standstill.

I finally arrived home, and my mother was sitting at the kitchen table holding her phone. "Come here, son," she said with a soft voice. I instantly became aggravated because I was in no mood to be lectured or criticized. "Not now, ma. I can't argue today," I said as I walked towards my room.

She said, "the doctor called." I stopped and turned back towards her and said, "For what? For who?" She looked at me

and said, "For me. I've been diagnosed with dementia." I had no idea what dementia was, nor did I know the severity of it. "So, are they giving you medication to cure it?" I asked. My mother looked at me and grabbed my hand, and said, "dementia is the beginning stages of Alzheimer's Disease.
There is no cure, son." I felt frozen. I was shocked by the news and ashamed of my attitude.

 We held each other as we cried for what seemed like hours. She was the only person in the world that truly loved me. She loved me when I was undeserving. I wasn't ready to watch my loving mother's mind slowly deteriorate until nothing was familiar to her. The thought that one day I'll be a stranger to her frightened me. Knowing one day, I'll have to introduce myself to the woman who gave me life 40 years ago tortured my mind.

I went with my mother to her first doctor's appointment since the diagnosis. The doctor sat down with my mother and me as he began speaking in medical terms, which my mother nor I understood. "Listen, doc, we need you to be completely honest with us. How bad is it?" I said as I held my mother's hand.

The doctor took a deep breath and said, *"Within a year and a half, she'll begin to forget simple things like her car keys, glasses, food on the stove, and things she may have thought about minutes before. The disease will begin to progress, and she'll start to forget people she's known for years. Smells and songs may temporarily bring her memory back, and she'll seem like she's getting better, but her memory will once again disappear. Eventually, everything she once knew and loved, such as people, places, and things, will become completely new to her, and she won't recognize them. By year 3 she'll forget things like eating, and she'll appear like an empty shell of herself. Unfortunately, one day you'll try to wake her, and she'll be....."*

A Mother's Love A Son's Regret

There was an awkward silence in the room. I squeezed my mother's hand like a scared little boy.

"I'll leave you two alone to process it all. I'm sorry", said the doctor as she left the room.

My body felt numb. This was worst than when the judge sentenced me to 15 years in prison. I felt lost. My mother wrapped her short arms around me and said, "Everything will be fine. It's ok to cry and feel sad now, but then it's back to living life. I only have a short time left, and we'll make the best of it." I hugged her as tight as I could and said, "I love you, mommy." It's amazing; no matter how old a man gets, fear will have him run back to his mother's arms.

The next few weeks were quiet. My mother didn't speak much at all. She would make a cup of coffee in the morning, and before she left for work, she'll leave a note that read,

"Son, I love you. Be happy today and read Romans 8:28."

I opened the old Bible on the table, and the scripture read,

"And we know that all things work together for good to them that love God, to them who are the called according to his purpose" (Romans 8:28).

I read that scripture every day, trying to make sense of everything that was going wrong in my life. Where was the good in my mother losing her ability to remember? Where was the good in going to prison for 13 years just to come home to unemployment? I didn't understand that scripture and why my mother believed in it so much, but she wrote the same scripture in her notes she left for me every morning.

One night, while my mother was in bed reading, I laid next to her. For the first few minutes, neither of us spoke. My mother then broke the silence and said,

"There will be a time when I may not remember things. Birthdays, your name,

*and even your face won't be familiar. I
may speak to you as if you are a stranger
but always remember I love you. As my
mind begins to dwindle away, my love for
you will be forever. When those days
arrive, I need you to be strong and
remember what I've just told you."*

I cried myself to sleep in my mother's
arms that night.
The following day my mother burst into
my room yelling, "Hurry! Get up and pack
your bags we're going on a vacation!"
What was she talking about? We just
received the worst news of our lives, and
she's excited and happy, like the day I
was released from prison. "Ma, are you
ok?" I asked. "I'm fine, son. I've worked
my entire life, and it's time to live. Get
your things packed, we're traveling the
world," my mother said. I'd never been
anywhere, so I was very excited.

The first place we went was to Florida.
We spent a week in Disney World. We've
never laughed and eaten so much in our
lives. We took pictures with Mickey and
Goofy. We ate at the Rain Forest Cafe'.
We got on roller coasters we would have

never imagined we'd ride.

"Where are we going next, Ma?"
I impatiently asked, "Las Vegas!" She
said as she screamed with excitement.
Those 3 days in Vegas were incredible.
We stayed at the MGM Grand Hotel. We
ate, laughed, and gambled small amounts
of money. We went to a Celine Dion
show, which was absolutely amazing.
My mother won $5,000 at a blackjack
table. I didn't even know she knew how to
play. She loved the lights and the fancy
cars that drove up and down the Vegas
strip. I've never seen her so happy.

After our last day in Vegas, my mother
says, "Cali, here we come!"We spent 2
days in Los Angeles, California. We saw
the stars on the Hollywood walk of fame.
My mother took a picture next to Denzel
Washington's star.
We went to the Staples Center and
watched Kobe Bryant and the Lakers play
against Lebron James, Dwyane Wade,
and the Miami Heat. We walked down the
famous Rodeo Drive. The shades my
mother wore would have made strangers

think she was a movie star. She deserved all of the happiness she felt at that moment.

I walked around with a notepad writing everything down. My mother would often say, "Boy, what are you writing in that book?" I would say to her, "Just keep enjoying yourself. You're going to make this book a bestseller."

We would eventually travel to Hawaii, London, Italy, Paris, Spain, China, Egypt, and Germany. I wrote down every moment. We saw Volcanoes, pyramids, The Eiffel Tower, The Queen of England, and The Great Wall Of China. Not bad for a single mother and her ex-con son. That was the best two months of our lives. Nothing mattered at that moment. We just laughed, ate, and laughed some more.

On our flight back home, my mother looked out of her first-class window smiling from ear to ear. She was at the happiest time of her life. My happiness was slowly beginning to fade, and reality was settling in. I knew the worst days were yet to come.

The months that followed are difficult to describe. It was now May 2012, 8 months since my mother's diagnosis. I began to see the beginning stages of her dementia slowly sneaking in. I noticed small things that my mother was forgetting. She would say good morning 5 times before she would go to work. She would leave me two identical notes on the kitchen table as if she totally forgot the first note she wrote. She would leave her car running outside, forgetting to turn off the ignition. The sad part about it all my mother thought the disease was moving slow, but she had no idea that it had already begun.

I often wrote my feeling down in my notebook. The mother that was by my side throughout the most challenging times in my life now needed me to try to repay an incredible debt of love. How do I care for my caregiver? I often prayed for guidance and wisdom. These were uncharted waters for me. I was still trying to take care of myself.

My mother's condition seemed to worsen every month. She still remembered who I

A Mother's Love A Son's Regret

was at this point, but everything else was slowly vanishing from her memory.

It was then 10 months since her diagnosis when she asked me, "Has it started yet? Do I forget things?"

I wanted to tell her the truth. I wanted to say to her for the past 2 months, her condition was becoming worst. But why? Why did she need to know she was slowly losing everything? Would it have helped her to know?

I told her, "Ma, you're doing great. Keep living your life." She smiled as if she were beating the disease.

I may have given her a false sense of hope, but I gave her hope by any means necessary.

Some may be reading this and thinking I was wrong for lying. Maybe you're right. Perhaps I should have told my mother the truth, but I didn't. I hope God forgave me for at least that one lie.

Each month was worse than the last.
My mother stopped eating on her own.
I began spoon-feeding her breakfast, lunch, and dinner.
She became like a toddler who needed

me for everything. It was my honor to care for her.

A year and a half had passed, and I was now a stranger to my own mother. Many of my friends told me I should place her in a nursing home. They told me I was giving up years of my life taking care of my sick mother. This loving woman took care of me for over 40 years. Scrapes and bruises as a toddler, she was there. Thirteen years in prison, and she never missed a visit. Through all of my rebellion and disrespect, she never stopped loving me. So I decided to stay by her side until the end.

She would sing "Amazing Grace" as she sat in her chair staring out of the living room window. That seemed to be the only thing she could remember consistently. I would sit with her for hours and sing along with her. I wanted every last moment I could grab.

One afternoon while I was fixing the sheets on her bed, I found a folded paper under her pillow. I unfolded the paper, and it read...

Dear Son,

I know by now the disease has taken its toll on me. I sit alone in a chair, a shell of my once self. I look at you now like I've never seen you in my entire life. But I need you to forget about what you see and remember what you know. Momma loves you more than life itself. All I ever wanted was the best for you. I may have been hard on you and upset you at times, but true love hurts. Don't worry about me, son. I'll be ok. Life is a journey, and we all are just passing through. I need you to promise me something. Publish what you've been writing in your notebook. Sorry, I've read a little bit a few months back. Turn your pain into prosperity. Have no regrets concerning me, son. I've already forgotten it...lol ...too soon? Just a little joke. Anyway, keep writing, son. Keep praying, living, and laughing. I love you forever. -Mom

PS- Read Philippians 4:7

The following day April 4th, 2013, my mother died laying in my arms. I held her lifeless body for 3 hours before I called the ambulance. She was 67 years old.

4 years later, I fulfilled my promise to her and published my first book, "A Mother's Love, A Son's Regret." The book would eventually sell millions of copies worldwide.

To all of the mother's reading this story, we appreciate you. As young men, we don't realize the magnitude of a mother's love until we are desperate for it.

A mother would lay down her life for her child. She would cross the largest oceans and walk through the deepest valleys to ensure her baby's safety.

From all the sons around the world, we say, "Thank you, Ma."

I've Got A Story To Tell
Poems By Corey Porter

I'm walking through life now
but my purpose is flying.
Life is much more than
working and dying.
May all of my good deeds leave prints
from my feet.
My struggles are puzzle pieces
yet to complete whom I'll be.

Dreams don't come true.
Dreams won't come if you Just wait for
them.
Dreams are stubborn.
Dreams are meant to run to.
Don't expect Him or Her to run too...
Because as far as Dreams...
I'm sure He or Her has one too...

And watching you chase your Dreams...
reminds them that their Dreams run
loose.

Don't Expect Opened Doors.
You'll Shiver Waiting For Chivalry.
Never Try To Break Open Jaws...
To Get Out The Word Of Mouth.
Never Force Hands To Applaud...
Haters Will Still Ignore What They've
Heard About.

Some Rather Show Their Shine...
Than Share It.
Some Rather Criticize...
Than Hear It.
Some Go From "I Need Ya' To Amnesia.
They'll Forget The Days You've Swiped
Visas.
It's The Weight Of A Giver.
Bear It.

Contact the Author

Instagram:@CoreyPorternet

Twitter:@CoreyPorter

Website: WritingsByCoreyPorter.com

Email: WritingsByCoreyPorter@gmail.com

Read it. Share It.

Corey Porter

40983358R00019